Highlights™
Hidden Pictures®

101

Socks

Knock your socks off by finding 101 hidden socks in these puzzles.

HIGHLIGHTS PRESS
Honesdale, Pennsylvania

Disco Owls

7 socks

heart

radish

paper clip

tack

shuttlecock

slice of pizza

hammer

rolling pin

crescent moon

pencil

drinking straw

piece of candy

lollipop

ice-cream bar

Art by Neil Numberman

Bunny Treehouse

sock

button

bell

adhesive bandage

fried egg

mitten

arrow

slice of pizza

fish

top hat

lemon

cane

horseshoe

envelope

heart

Art Lesson

sock

boomerang

olive

boot

golf club

mitten

flashlight

Art by Bill Golliher

teacup

funnel

comb

needle

doughnut

closed
umbrella

ladle

pennant

lightning
bolt

ruler

hockey
stick

crown

canoe

paper
airplane

Dino Discovery

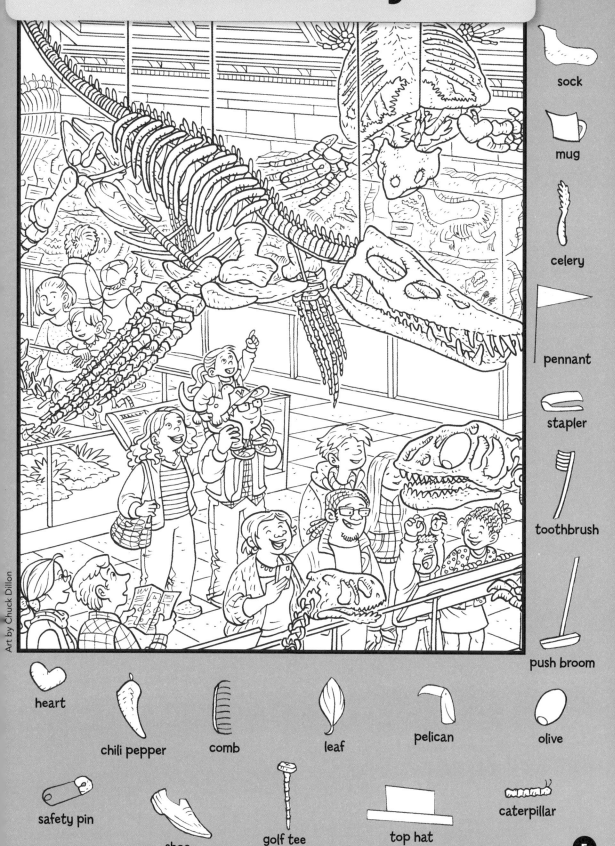

sock

mug

celery

pennant

stapler

toothbrush

push broom

heart

chili pepper

comb

leaf

pelican

olive

safety pin

shoe

golf tee

top hat

caterpillar

Art by Chuck Dillon

Mana-tea Party

sock

wristwatch

saltshaker

lemon

bird

crescent moon

apple core

knitted hat

butterfly

fan

glove

screw

pennant

bowl

caterpillar

lollipop

toothbrush

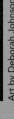

Art by Deborah Johnson

Camp Out

sock

ice-cream bar

candle

mug

starfish

carrot

heart

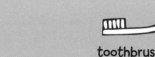
toothbrush

slice of pie

pennant

glove

bowl

Art by Mary Sullivan

7

Dinosaur Day

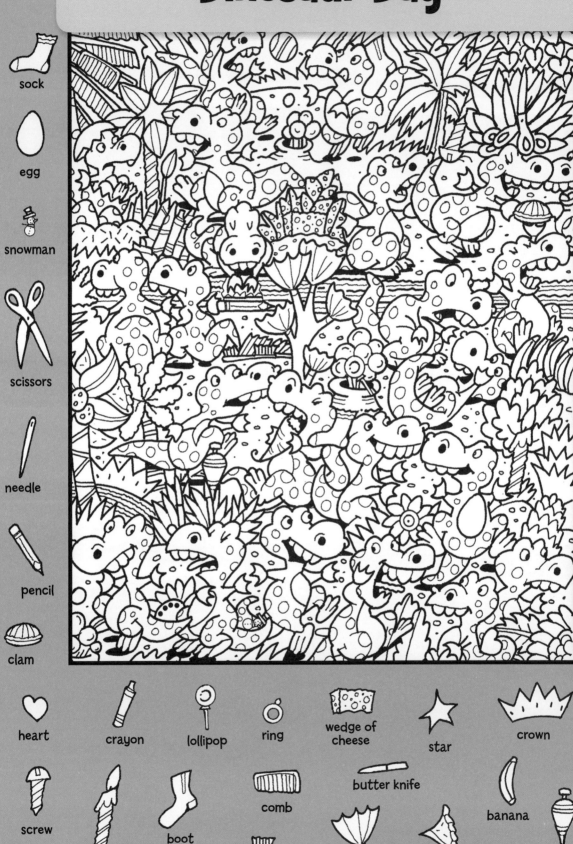

sock

egg

snowman

scissors

needle

pencil

clam

heart

crayon

lollipop

ring

wedge of cheese

star

crown

screw

candle

boot

comb

toothbrush

butter knife

fan

slice of pie

banana

top

Art by Diana Zourelias

Bee-Ball

sock

ring

key

teacup

heart

bell

banana

plate

nail

fish

shoe

horn

bird

Art by Tim Davis

Toad-eo

sock

crescent moon

heart

tweezers

egg

teacup

worm

pencil

ice-cream cone

banana

eyeglasses

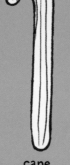
cane

fish

duck

Art by Tim Davis

Backyard Talent Show

sock

crescent moon

flag

slice of watermelon

doughnut

slice of bread

ice-cream cone

chili pepper

crayon

megaphone

star

ruler

heart

wishbone

envelope

seashell

Rainy-Day Fun

sock

ring

toothbrush

spider

crescent moon

mitten

spoon

banana

flag

wishbone

umbrella

pointy hat

fish

Art by Karen Stormer-Brooks

Pirate School

sock

pear

lollipop

ice-cream cone

slice of pizza

canoe

book

needle

carrot

scissors

spoon

crown

envelope

doughnut

Frogs on Board

sock

flag

glove

hat

lollipop

bowl

crescent
moon

banana

Art by Laura Ferraro Close

Seal and Turtle

sock

cupcake

baseball bat

slice of pizza

baseball cap

slice of bread

spoon

house

vase

open book

banana

heart

mushroom

paper clip

tweezers

slice of pie

Art by Maggie Swanson

15

Penguin Pond

sock

paintbrush

needle

mushroom

crescent moon

Art by Rocky Fuller

pencil

hamburger

cherry

teacup

tack

heart

wedge of cheese

toothbrush

hot dog

flower

16

The Diner

sock

egg

needle

artist's brush

bell

tack

ring

wrench

comb

hockey stick

ice-cream bar

mushroom

candle

crescent moon

banana

closed umbrella

Art by Chuck Dillon

17

Frog Pond

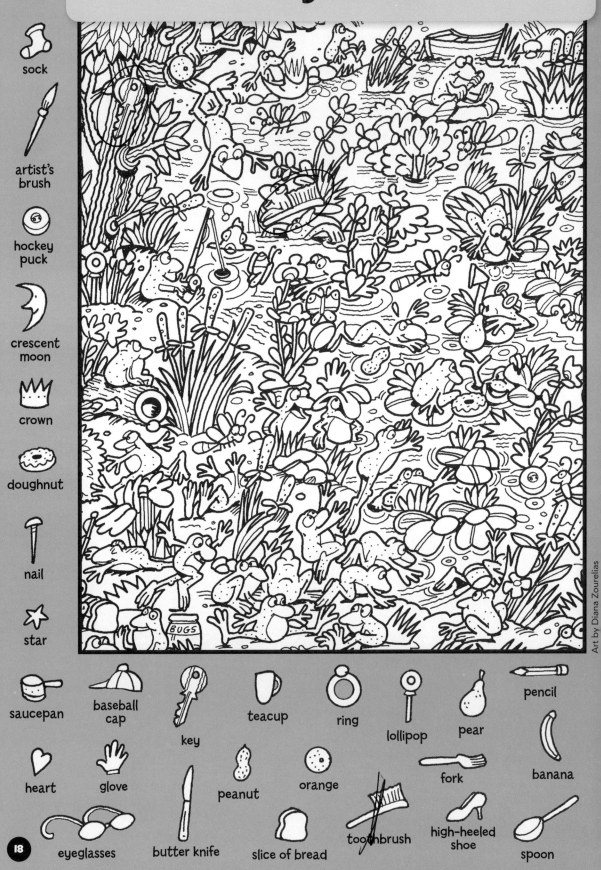

sock

artist's brush

hockey puck

crescent moon

crown

doughnut

nail

star

saucepan

baseball cap

key

teacup

ring

lollipop

pear

pencil

heart

glove

peanut

orange

fork

banana

eyeglasses

butter knife

slice of bread

toothbrush

high-heeled shoe

spoon

Art by Diana Zourelias

Summer Splash

sock

cactus

slice of
pizza

cane

fried egg

needle

hairbrush

rolling pin

heart

wedge of
orange

yo-yo

crayon

party hat

present

mitten

Art by Deborah Johnson

19

Alive Hive

sock

bell

kite

fish

coat hanger

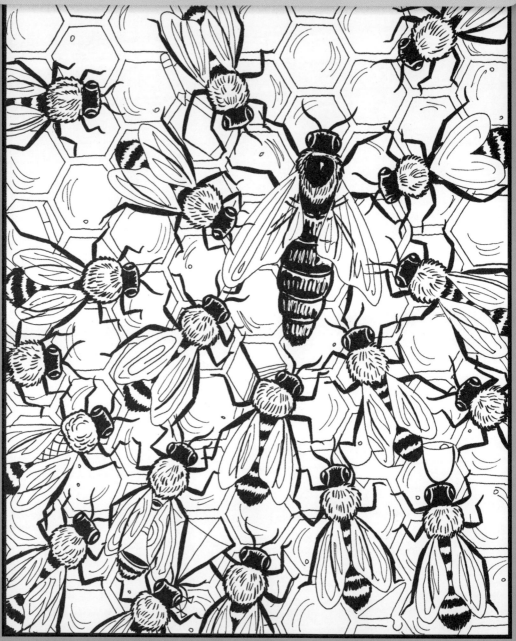

Art by Tim Davis

heart

needle

pencil

ice-cream cone

horn

open book

paper clip

sailboat

20

Starship Cheese

sock

needle

rolling pin

balloon

banana

crescent moon

Art by David Galchutt

apple

candy cane

cookie

carrot

doughnut

closed umbrella

bowling ball

fish

ring

candle

comb

21

Big-Top Beetles

sock

crescent moon

toothbrush

mitten

broccoli

ring

spoon

candle

musical notes

whale

bird

ax

wedge of lemon

magnifying glass

shovel

slice of pizza

candy cane

Art by Pat Lewis

Dancing Bears

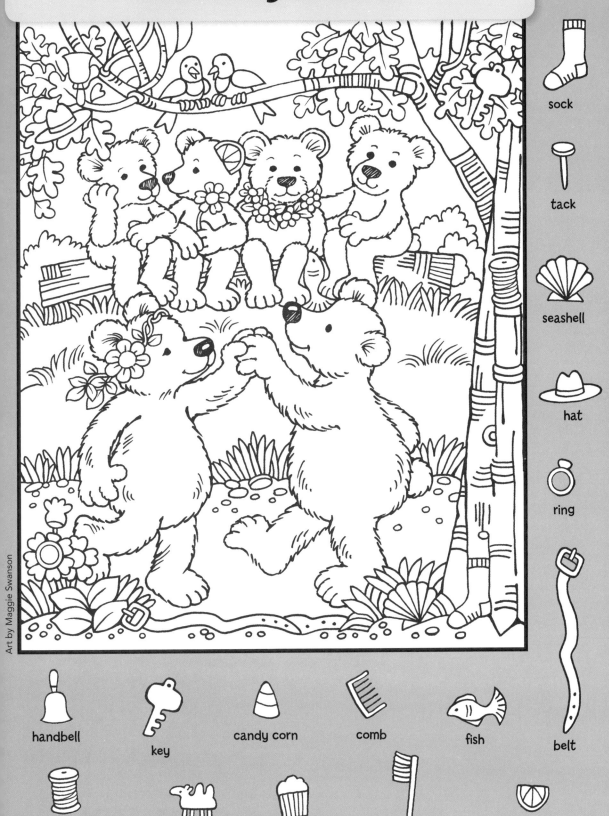

Art by Maggie Swanson

sock

tack

seashell

hat

ring

belt

handbell

key

candy corn

comb

fish

spool of thread

camel

muffin

toothbrush

wedge of lemon

Paddle Pals

sock

cane

teacup

open book

heart

pennant

fishhook

pencil

palm tree

whistle

postage stamp

ice-cream bar

artist's brush

ruler

puzzle piece

snowman

mushroom

drinking glass with straw

slice of pizza

closed umbrella

saltshaker

Art by Jennifer Harney

24

Renaissance Cat

sock

fried egg

golf club

sailboat

banana

chef's hat

horseshoe

kite

bow tie

necklace

slice of bread

slice of pie

paintbrush

ring

envelope

ladle

button

hockey stick

snake

ax

Art by David Helton

Hieroglyphics

sock

toothbrush

button

crescent moon

cherry

comb

candle

crown

artist's brush

tube of toothpaste

mug

bell

acorn

golf club

saltshaker

tack

banana

baseball cap

ring

Art by Mike DeSantis

Big Frog Band

sock

bell

crescent moon

knitted hat

sailboat

spatula

boot

crown

glove

seashell

heart

teacup

flowerpot

mallet

slice of pie

scissors

butter knife

Art by Gary Mohrman

Block Party

sock
banana
bell
screwdriver
bow
paper clip
lollipop
cane
flag
crescent moon
heart
pencil
book
glove
envelope
nail
light bulb
cupcake
crown
magnet
teacup
slice of pizza
button
ice-cream cone
ruler

Art by Alison Hertz

Soup for Lunch

sock

fishhook

crayon

top hat

ring

slice of bread

iron

lollipop

tack

butterfly

trowel

magnet

mitten

Beaver Construction Crew

sock

butter knife

crescent moon

paper clip

candle

envelope

wishbone

toothbrush

tack

spoon

paintbrush

seashell

ring

chili pepper

crown

paper airplane

fried egg

Art by Gary Mohrman

Happy Birthday!

sock

paper clip

lampshade

mallet

ice-cream cone

slice of pizza

ice skate

crescent moon

doughnut

ring

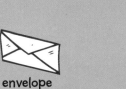
toothbrush

slipper

envelope

lock

Bus Stop

sock

carrot

ball of yarn

slice of cake

fan

wedge of lemon

button

dog bone

ruler

leaf

envelope

flashlight

artist's brush

horseshoe

pear

baby's rattle

mushroom

spool of thread

fried egg

American flag

fish

caterpillar

wedge of cheese

kite

32

Art by Marnie Gallacher-Cole

Rained Out

sock

toothbrush

spoon

banana

ice-cream bar

teacup

bell

feather

bowl

basket

mitten

golf club

pencil

ring

tack

ruler

Marching Band

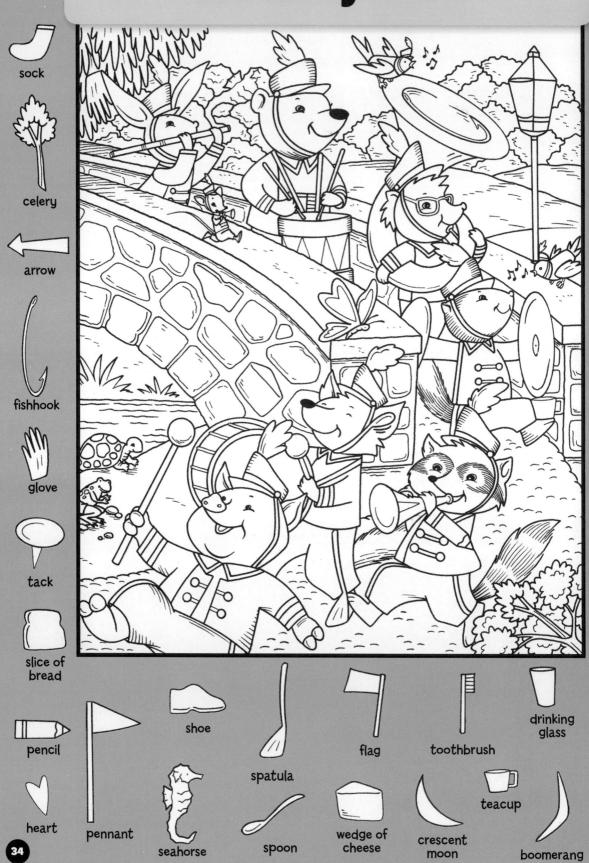

sock

celery

arrow

fishhook

glove

tack

slice of bread

pencil

heart

pennant

shoe

seahorse

spatula

spoon

flag

wedge of cheese

toothbrush

crescent moon

teacup

drinking glass

boomerang

Art by Gary Mohrman

Friendly Fairies

sock

carrot

crown

heart

ring

tomato

hot dog

mitten

crescent moon

muffin

fishhook

football

fried egg

banana

arrow

spoon

belt

purse

baseball cap

Art by Mernie Gallagher-Cole

35

Barn Dance

sock

building block

wristwatch

elf's hat

wedge of cheese

adhesive bandage

needle

arrow

tube of toothpaste

drinking straw

spatula

exclamation point

open book

pencil

candle

envelope

Art by Gary Mohrman

Monkeying Around

sock

paper clip

cane

mushroom

baseball cap

peanut

pennant

umbrella

artist's brush

olive

shoe

sailboat

heart

scissors

strawberry

zipper

glove

Art by Deborah Johnson

East Galaxy School

sock

light bulb

coin

banana

drinking glass

wedge of lemon

Art by Paula Becker

bowl

flashlight

slice of pie

fried egg

envelope

horseshoe

ring

doughnut

slice of watermelon

Animals at the Pool

sock

crescent moon

needle

lollipop

mug

hammer

toothbrush

artist's brush

cane

slice of pie

ring

spoon

telescope

leaf

sailboat

magnet

snake

pennant

funnel

heart

Art by Rocky Fuller

39

Super Swine

sock

bird

butter knife

mug

lock

fish

horn

fishhook

ruler

envelope

crescent moon

kite

cotton candy

drumstick

needle

can

piece of popcorn

stick of gum

dog bone

magician's wand

mushroom

flag

golf club

crown

button

hockey stick

olive

snow cone

adhesive bandage

SUPER SWINE NABS RASCALLY RODENT!

Art by Bill Golliher

40

Roof Garden

Art by Chuck Galey

sock

heart

candle

muffin

canoe

bowl

pencil

ruler

needle

open book

domino

sailboat

wishbone

glove

banana

toothbrush

nail

ring

fork

envelope

Hopscotch

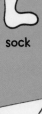
sock

envelope

teacup

crescent
moon

balloon

bell

sailboat

lightning
bolt

kite

wedge of
lemon

ice-cream
bar

ruler

comb

candle

slice of pizza

Art by Tamara Petrosino

Sea Life

sock

necklace

peanut

closed
umbrella

noisemaker

Art by Scot Ritchie

boomerang

drinking straw

eyeglasses

cowboy hat

exclamation
point

shovel

magnifying
glass

screw

mitten

cane

orange

piece of
candy

teardrop

teacup

rabbit

43

When Pigs Fly

sock

crescent moon

glove

four-leaf clover

comb

wristwatch

flower

mushroom

grapes

saltshaker

lock

heart

button

bird

duck

pear

owl

eyeglasses

Art by Diana Zourelias

Race to First Base

Art by Robert Peterson

sock

clothespin

candle

needle

pennant

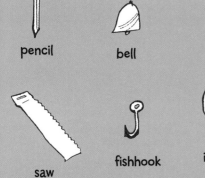

pencil

bell

fish

slice of pizza

nail

saw

fishhook

ice-cream cone

pear

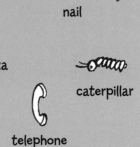

caterpillar

telephone receiver

feather

Diner Days

sock

mallet

sailboat

bell

umbrella

hockey stick

paper clip

sneaker

spatula

coat hanger

pencil

paper airplane

toothbrush

Art by Tim Davis

Animal Arcade

sock

spool of thread

traffic light

golf club

sailboat

candle

mushroom

saltshaker

needle

horseshoe

T-shirt

lollipop

ring

crown

bell

cherry

crescent moon

artist's brush

spoon

wedge of lemon

Art by Gary LaCoste

Baking Cookies

sock

penguin

flag

comb

feather

manatee

worm

tube of toothpaste

toothbrush

yo-yo

boomerang

sailboat

baseball bat

Art by Chuck Dillon

Snow Castle

sock

high-heeled shoe

candle

pear

doughnut

chili pepper

ice-cream cone

clam

pencil

pennant

drinking glass

heart

mushroom

funnel

cracker

slice of pie

crescent moon

Art by Gary Mohrman

Barrel of Monkeys

sock

worm

golf club

tube of
toothpaste

bell

pair of
shorts

pear

needle

wishbone

fishhook

slice of pie

mouse

hammer

Art by R. Michael Palan

Tadpoles

sock

ring

scissors

heart

crescent moon

bird

feather

duck

artist's brush

fork

ice-cream cone

paper clip

toothbrush

spoon

Bookworm

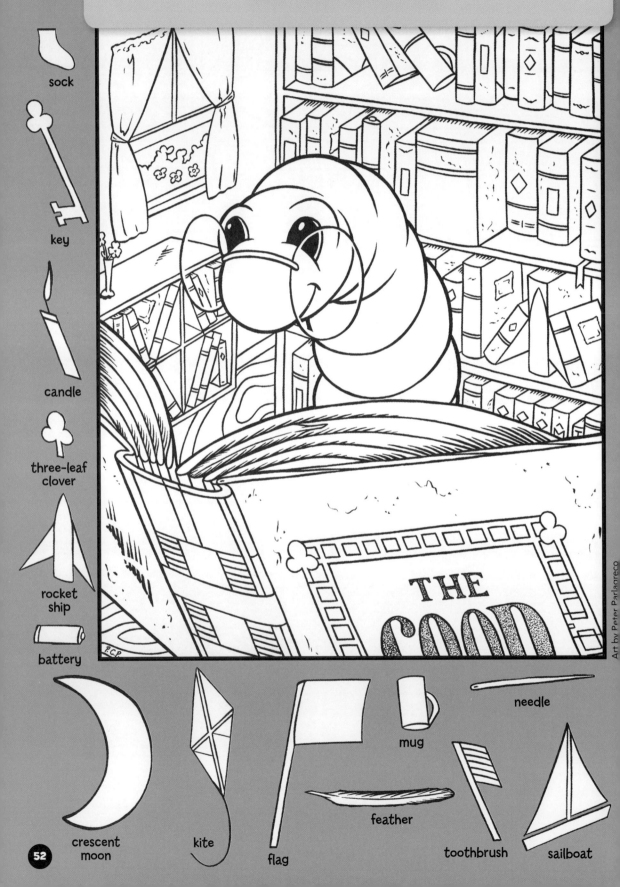

sock

key

candle

three-leaf clover

rocket ship

battery

crescent moon

kite

flag

feather

mug

needle

toothbrush

sailboat

THE GOOD

Art by Peter Parlagreco

Bird Bath

Art by Tim Davis

sock

paper clip

crescent moon

glove

toothbrush

snail

heart

star

pencil

banana

slice of pie

fish

nail

sailboat

53

Playground Paradise

sock

teacup

artist's brush

needle

crown

spool of thread

mushroom

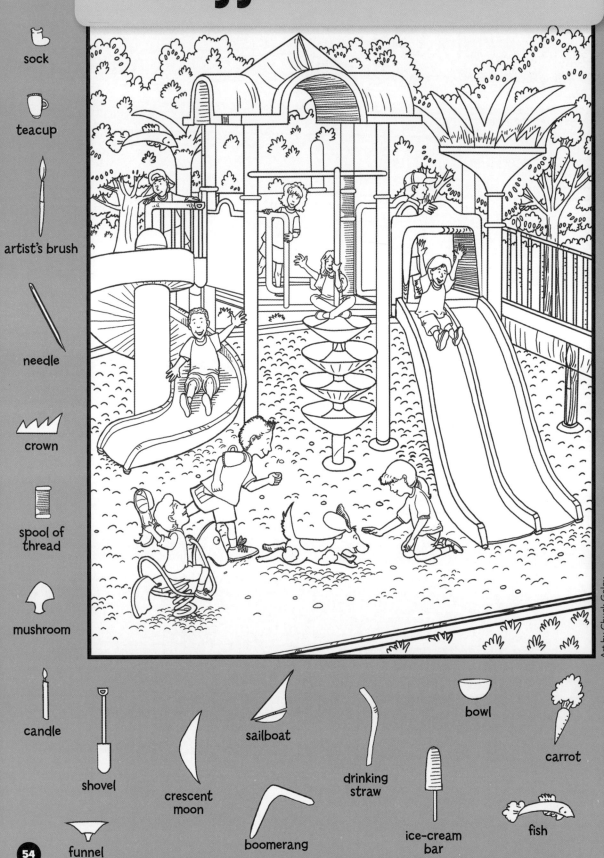

Art by Chuck Galey

candle

shovel

crescent moon

sailboat

boomerang

drinking straw

ice-cream bar

bowl

carrot

fish

funnel

Moving Day

Art by Mary Sullivan

sock

book

fire hydrant

spoon

crayon

drinking straw

teacup

shoe

saucepan

slice of pizza

sailboat

ice-cream bar

pennant

magnet

fishhook

closed umbrella

toothbrush

Bunnies Blowing Bubbles

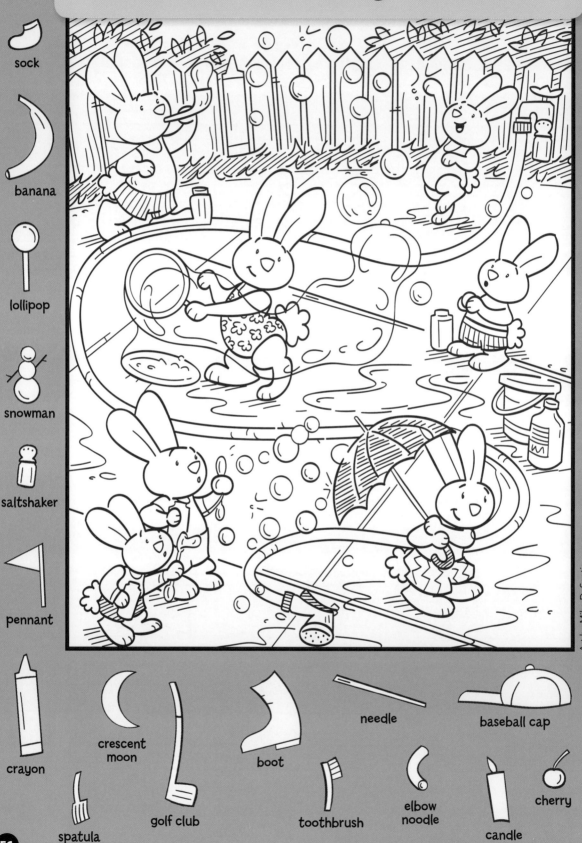

sock

banana

lollipop

snowman

saltshaker

pennant

crayon

crescent moon

golf club

spatula

boot

toothbrush

needle

elbow noodle

candle

baseball cap

cherry

Art by Mike DeSantis

Silly Statues

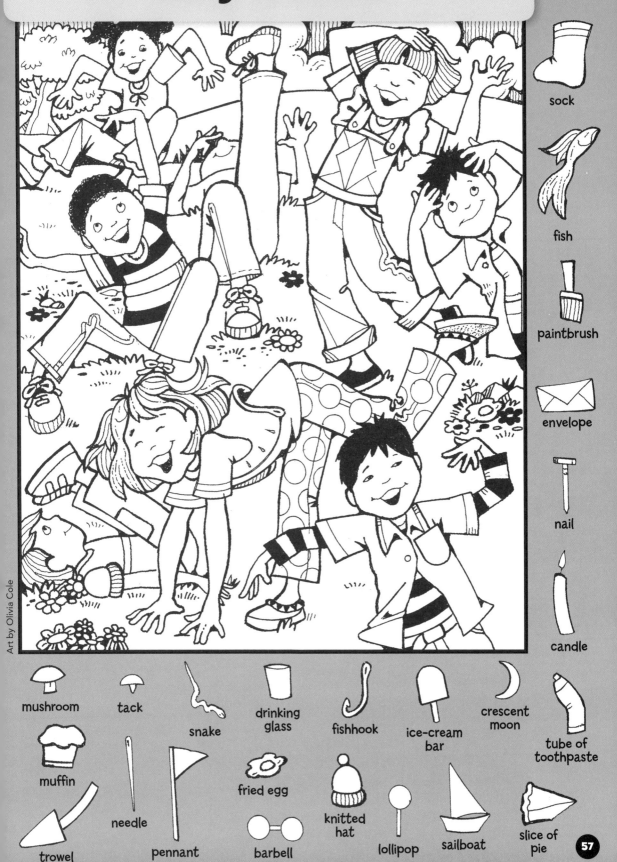

Art by Olivia Cole

sock

fish

paintbrush

envelope

nail

candle

mushroom

tack

snake

drinking glass

fishhook

ice-cream bar

crescent moon

tube of toothpaste

muffin

needle

pennant

fried egg

barbell

knitted hat

lollipop

sailboat

slice of pie

trowel

Garden Bugs

sock

crescent moon

fish

crown

slice of cake

balloon

scissors

bell

artist's brush

slice of watermelon

teacup

hot dog

lollipop

cupcake

banana

hamburger

baseball bat

sun

paper clip

canoe

football

Art by Mernie Gallagher-Cole

Big Fish

sock

slice of watermelon

iron

trowel

paintbrush

banana

flag

bell

tennis ball

boot

cactus

knitted hat

candle

clothespin

soccer ball

pencil

Art by Patrick Girouard

Spring Dance

sock

megaphone

heart

teacup

funnel

baseball glove

wristwatch

vase

clam

needle

tack

artist's brush

spoon

slice of pie

pennant

carrot

Art by Gary Mohrman

Dino Wonder

Art by Catherine Copeland

sock

artist's brush

bowling ball

candy corn

needle

olive

heart

star

baseball bat

domino

snow cone

Winter Friend

sock

pear

balloon

ice-cream
cone

baseball
bat

Art by Jim Hunt

ghost

comb

fork

crescent
moon

star

letter

dog bone

baseball

glove

cherry

Dinosaur Museum

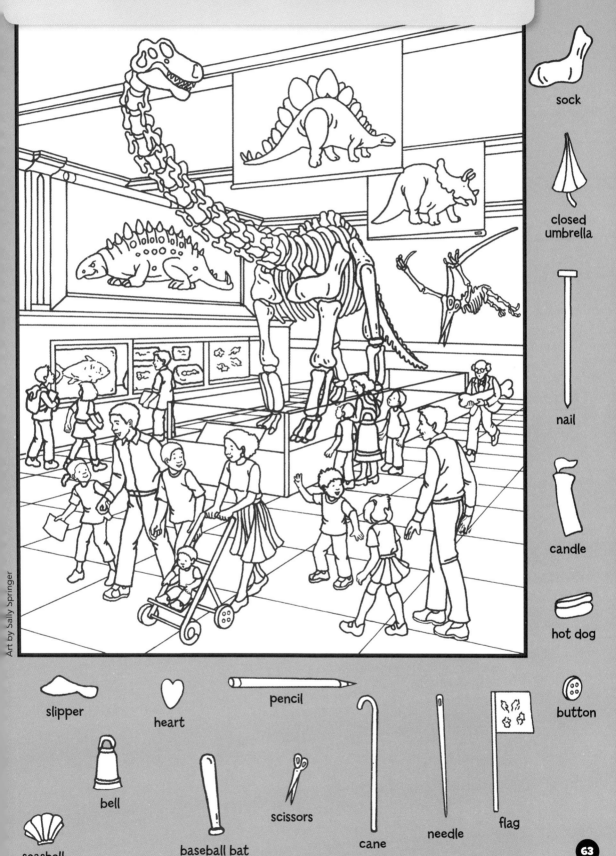

sock

closed umbrella

nail

candle

hot dog

button

slipper

heart

pencil

cane

needle

flag

bell

scissors

seashell

baseball bat

Art by Sally Springer

Coral Reef Library

sock

candle

paintbrush

spoon

safety pin

wishbone

crescent moon

teapot

funnel

needle

banana

artist's brush

sailboat

slice of bread

ladybug

ring

Art by Chuck Galey

The Great Big Pumpkin

Art by Olivia Cole

sock

crescent moon

flag

slice of pizza

bowl

drinking straw

mushroom

banana

boot

toothbrush

candle

pear

tube of toothpaste

dove

ring

ice-cream bar

slice of cake

snail

crayon

trowel

tack

mug

handbell

funnel

knitted hat

snake

Sing-Along

sock

heart

pen

tube of
toothpaste

Art by Diana Zourelias

bell

button

insect

magnifying
glass

Foxes in the Garden

sock

bell

spool of thread

seashell

artist's brush

crescent moon

arrow

ring

flag

slice of bread

pencil

lollipop

spatula

envelope

slice of pie

shovel

fish

crayon

needle

thimble

Art by Gary Mohrman

Snow Angels

sock

fishhook

toothbrush

needle

saltshaker

crescent moon

bell

paper clip

spoon

fork

flashlight

mug

Art by Jennifer Emery

Fish Friends

sock

pair of pants

pencil

artist's brush

glove

mitten

butterfly

closed umbrella

cupcake

spoon

crescent moon

fountain pen

drumstick

Art by Susan T. Hall

Fiesta del Mar

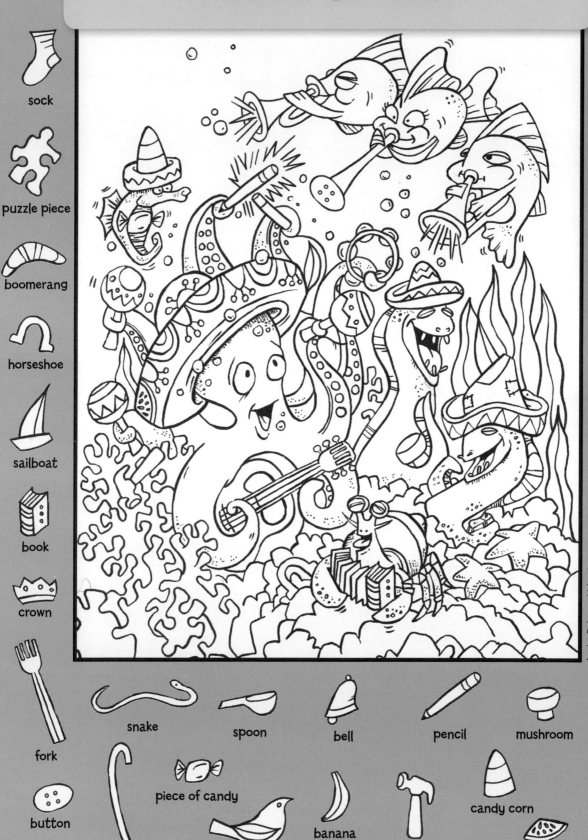

sock

puzzle piece

boomerang

horseshoe

sailboat

book

crown

fork

button

snake

spoon

bell

pencil

mushroom

piece of candy

cane

bird

banana

hammer

candy corn

slice of watermelon

Art by Rebecca Valentine

Bear Grills

sock

bell

slice of pie

wedge of lemon

button

pennant

artist's brush

feather

hockey stick

envelope

candle

golf club

tack

muffin

glove

spool of thread

Art by David Helton

Beachcombers

sock

button

crescent moon

teddy bear

strawberry

ladle

hat

muffin

handbell

hairbrush

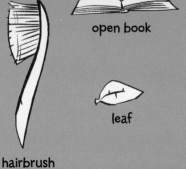
open book

leaf

banana

saw

dinosaur

Art by Laura Freeman

Swine Lake

sock

mushroom

slice of watermelon

ice-cream cone

scissors

hamburger

yo-yo

fishhook

bat

tomato

party hat

candy cane

canoe

spoon

crayon

dog bone

jump rope

belt

crescent moon

hat

rainbow

Art by Mernie Gallagher-Cole

73

Shark Tank

sock

tooth

spatula

glove

crescent moon

key

chef's hat

bell

ice-cream cone

funnel

ghost

elbow noodle

broccoli

piece of popcorn

gingerbread man

Art by Laura Ferraro Close

Rock Climbing

sock

turtle

candy corn

seashell

fishhook

sailboat

apple

mug

magnifying glass

ladybug

acorn

ring

boomerang

fish

mitten

wishbone

Art by Chuck Dillon

Swimming Lesson

sock

banana

worm

crescent moon

slice of watermelon

canoe

shuttlecock

paintbrush

megaphone

crown

table-tennis paddle

fishhook

pennant

musical note

ghost

needle

Art by Scot Ritchie

Pumpkin Patch

Art by Chuck Galey

sock

baseball bat

paintbrush

closed umbrella

banana

crescent moon

artist's brush

comb

nail

boomerang

fish

carrot

needle

slice of pie

ghost

Nature Sketchbook

sock

boot

slice of pie

fried egg

football

saltshaker

Art by Nuno Alexandre Vieira

bell

teacup

ghost

paper clip

pennant

crescent
moon

ice-cream
bar

muffin

fish

Parade Riders

sock

slice of pie

ruler

piece of popcorn

seashell

ice-cream cone

snake

shovel

teardrop

megaphone

spool of thread

pencil

crown

crescent moon

needle

hairpin

Art by Apryl Stott

Butterflies and Flowers

sock

comb

eyeglasses

candle

carrot

artist's brush

saltshaker

slice of pizza

pen

button

frying pan

hot dog

slipper

plate

banana

closed umbrella

ice-cream bar

necktie

ice-cream cone

spoon

pencil

baseball bat

Art by Lyn Martin

The One That Got Away

sock

extension cord

pennant

comb

banana

saw

pencil

slice of pie

trowel

bottle

fried egg

apple

frying pan

iron

paper clip

slice of pizza

cupcake

Art by Joe Kulka

Rainy-Day Reading

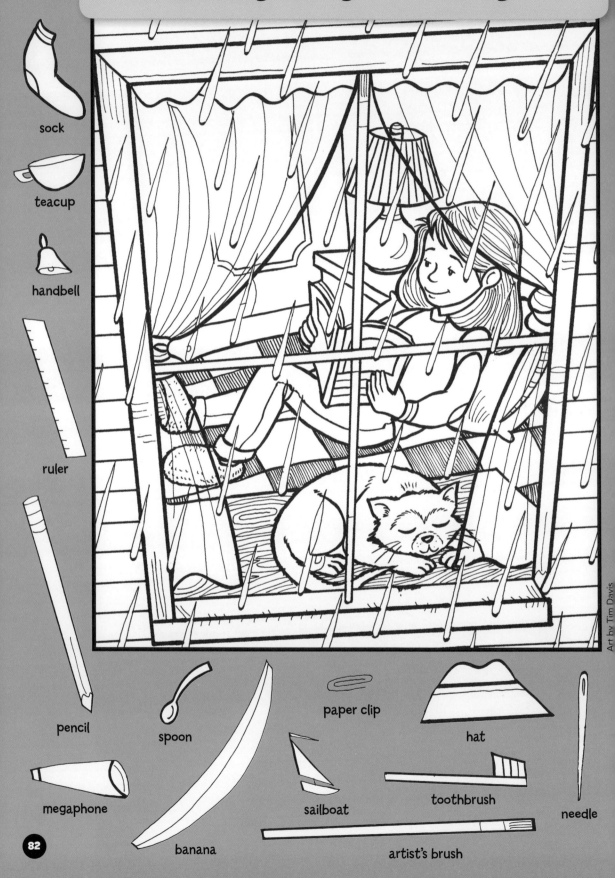

sock

teacup

handbell

ruler

pencil

spoon

megaphone

banana

paper clip

sailboat

artist's brush

hat

toothbrush

needle

Art by Tim Davis

Ice Sculpting

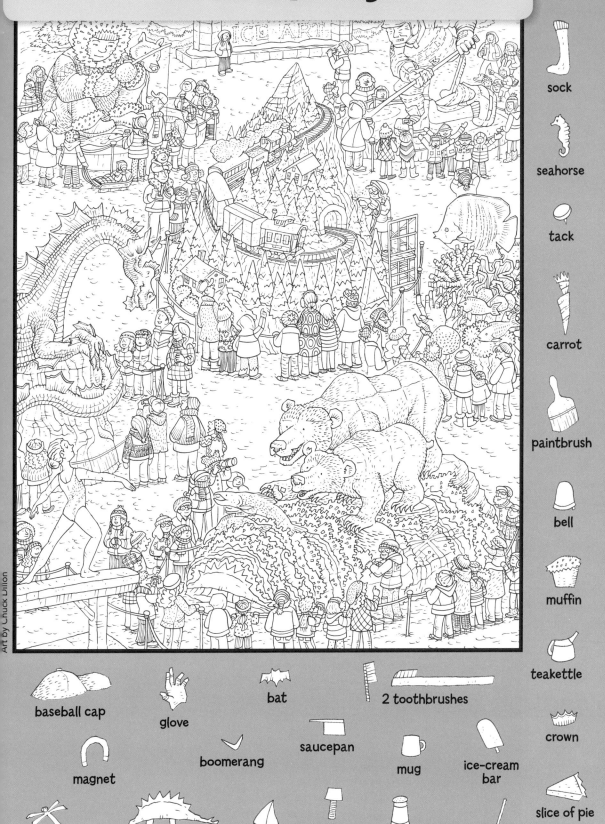

sock

seahorse

tack

carrot

paintbrush

bell

muffin

teakettle

crown

slice of pie

baseball cap

glove

bat

2 toothbrushes

saucepan

mug

ice-cream bar

magnet

boomerang

dragonfly

dinosaur

sailboat

lamp

saltshaker

golf club

Go Long!

sock

badge

button

paper clip

banana

key

wristwatch

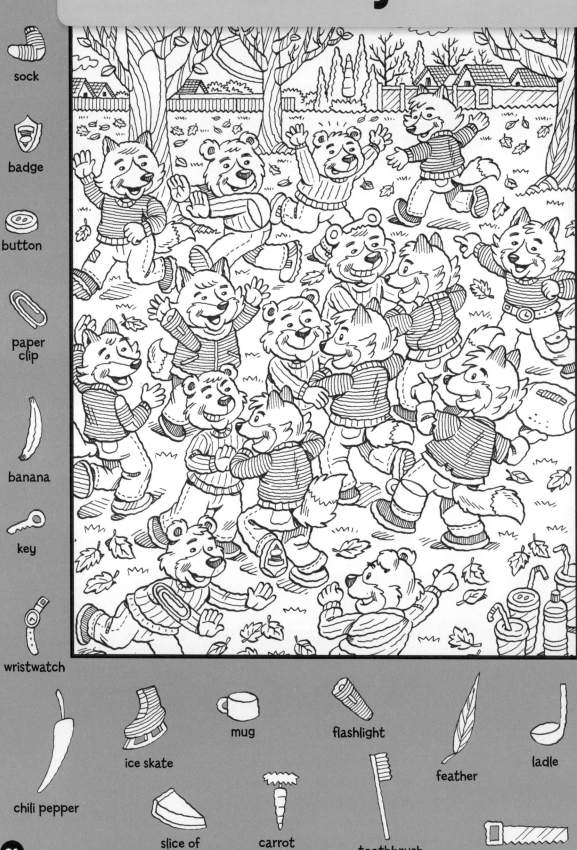

Art by David Helton

chili pepper

ice skate

slice of pie

mug

carrot

flashlight

toothbrush

feather

ladle

saw

Insect Serenade

sock

artist's brush

car

thermometer

paper clip

slice of cake

lollipop

drinking straw

mitten

slice of bread

slice of pizza

necktie

banana

Art by Karen Stormer-Brooks

Play in the Park

sock

magnifying glass

bell

slice of bacon

carrot

bowl

spatula

hammer

wristwatch

artist's brush

ruler

slice of pie

pencil

needle

snowman

snake

spoon

mitten

book

Art by Lyn Martin

Garden Visitors

Art by Maggie Swanson

sock

banana

spoon

baseball glove

teacup

apple core

toothbrush

gingerbread man

pencil

artist's brush

heart

slice of pizza

fish

open book

Catch!

sock

trowel

key

comb

star

toothbrush

pushpin

shoe

glove

heart

banana

light bulb

fish

lollipop

spoon

crescent moon

fishhook

artist's brush

bell

bowl

sailboat

strawberry

thimble

safety pin

Art by Leighanne Schneider

Aerial View

sock

domino

crayon

teacup

fish

adhesive bandage

pencil

ice-cream cone

party hat

wedge of lemon

snowman

snake

snow cone

ball of yarn

slice of pizza

Penguin Posing

sock

lightning bolt

musical note

candy corn

yo-yo

bell

boomerang

oar

mushroom

flag

slice of bread

spool of thread

potato

drumstick

hot dog

elf's hat

arrow

funnel

Art by Laura Ferraro Close

Lovebirds

Canoeing with Dad

sock

flag

muffin

potato

hamburger

heart

spool of thread

coat hanger

teacup

saw

scissors

sailboat

spoon

waffle

eyeglasses

apple

feather

ruler

Art by Marilee Herrald-Pilz

Planet Project

Art by Jennifer Harney

sock

paw print

traffic cone

banana

toothbrush

feather

lollipop

dragonfly

frying pan

snake

slice of pizza

musical note

candy cane

key

bowl

drinking glass with straw

bell

crown

snowman

clock

In the Water

sock

glove

banana

hockey stick

cane

nail

teacup

hat

mushroom

needle

snake

candle

tube of toothpaste

spatula

slice of pie

bow

Art by George Wildman

Family Vacation

Art by Tim Davis

sock

ruler

sailboat

clock

heart

toothbrush

star

teacup

dog

magnifying
glass

seal

glove

eyeglasses

saw

95

Splendid Salad

sock

paper clip

slice of bread

drinking straw

balloon

ice-cream bar

tack

slice of cake

crown

snail

paper airplane

mushroom

needle

mug

crescent moon

mallet

barbell

toothbrush

worm

ring

fishhook

Art by Olivia Cole

Sock and Roll!

Did you rock the socks off those puzzles by finding all 101 hidden socks? Don't worry, that's not the whole book. Those Hidden Pictures® puzzles are paired with a lot more fun for your sole enjoyment. But before you try on the other puzzles, answer these questions, looking back at the puzzles you just solved.

What other articles of clothing can you find?

Just like socks, both mittens and gloves usually come in pairs. Which can you find more of?

How many spools of thread can you find to patch up your old holey socks?

Sock It to 'Em

Hurricane Henry has hit Henry's bedroom. He needs seven pairs of socks to pack for camp. Can you help him find matches for the socks numbered 1 through 7?

Art by Kevin Rechin

Two of a Kind

Can you find the 2 sock monkeys that are the same?

Art by Clay Cantrell

Sock Drop

Find the correct route for this sock to make it down the laundry chute.

Art by Tom Woolley

Dressed-Up Jokes

Why don't bears wear socks?
They have bear feet.

Why did the Dalmatian wear
a striped shirt?
So he wouldn't be spotted

What do you call a dinosaur
wearing a cowboy hat?
Tyrannosaurus Tex

What do penguins wear
on their head?
Ice caps

Knock, knock.
Who's there?
Clothesline.
Clothesline who?
Clothesline all over the
floor end up wrinkled.

What are a ghost's
favorite pants?
Boo jeans

Why did the model wear
fancy clothes for her flight?
*Because she was going on
the runway*

What do reptiles wear
on their feet?
Snakers

Kara: My mom says that I get
to choose my school
clothes this year.
Sara: Oh, really? My dog's the
one that chews mine!

Fashion Find

There are 18 items of clothing hidden in this grid—up, down, across, backward, and diagonally. We found SOCKS. Can you find the rest?

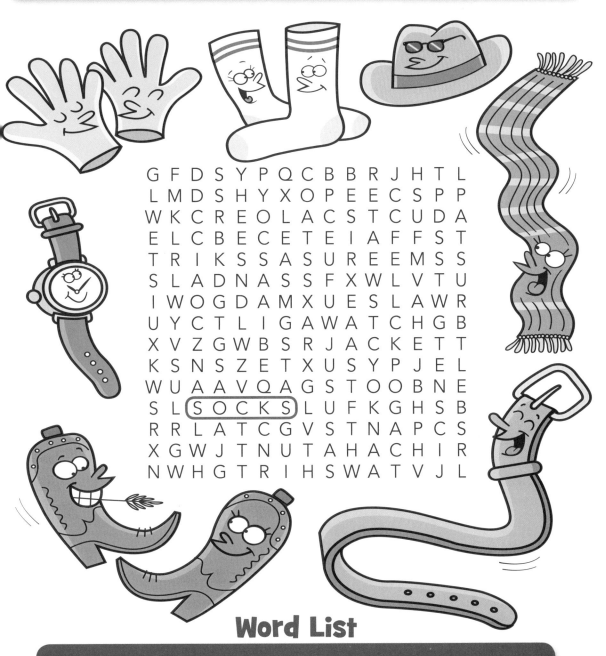

```
G F D S Y P Q C B B R J H T L
L M D S H Y X O P E E C S P P
W K C R E O L A C S T C U D A
E L C B E C E T E I A F F S T
T R I K S S A S U R E E M S S
S L A D N A S S F X W L V T U
I W O G D A M X U E S L A W R
U Y C T L I G A W A T C H G B
X V Z G W B S R J A C K E T T
K S N S Z E T X U S Y P J E L
W U A A V Q A G S T O O B N E
S L S O C K S L U F K G H S B
R R L A T C G V S T N A P C S
X G W J T N U T A H A C H I R
N W H G T R I H S W A T V J L
```

Word List

BELT	HAT	SHIRT	SWEATER
BOOTS	JACKET	SHOES	SWIMSUIT
COAT	PANTS	SKIRT	WATCH
DRESS	SANDALS	SOCKS	
GLOVES	SCARF	SUNGLASSES	

Crazy Sock Day

Leo and his friends each wore different socks for Crazy Sock Day. Using the clues below, can you figure out which socks each friend wore and what prize they won?

	Monkey Socks	Monster Socks	Popcorn Socks	Superhero Socks	Cow Socks	Best Overall	Most Creative	Silliest	Funniest	Scariest
Leo										
Hazel										
Wyatt										
Nora										
Eli										

**Use the chart to keep track of your answers.
Put an X in each box that can't be true and an O in boxes that match.**

1. The two girls each wore socks with animals on them.

2. Nora's and Wyatt's awards start with the same letter.

3. The kid who wore monkey socks won Best Overall.

4. Leo congratulated his friend who wore popcorn socks on his Silliest award.

5. Eli was excited that his superhero socks won Funniest.

Art by Mike Brownlow

Check . . . and Double Check

Compare these two pictures. Can you find at least 16 differences?

Art by Roz Fulcher

Sock Shop

David is buying socks for his twin brothers. Help him find 2 pairs of white socks that match exactly.

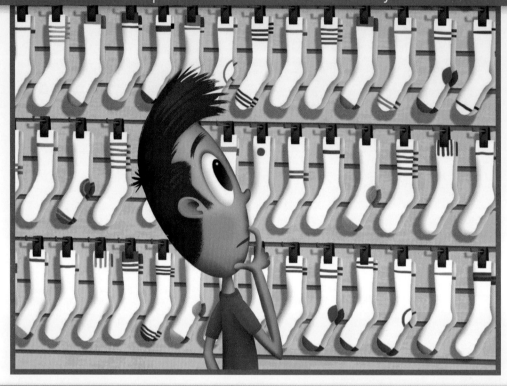

Art by Kevin Zimmer

Sock Designs

Create your own design on the sock below.

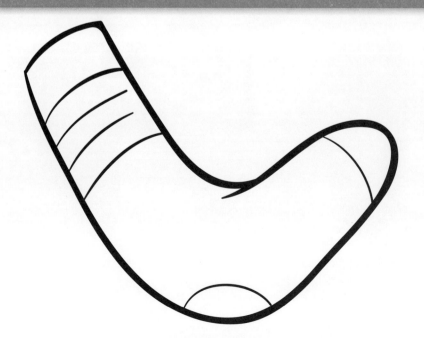

Art by Jennifer Harney

Pirate's Code

Captain Achilles keeps losing his mates—his sock's mates, that is! In order to keep them clean, he threw them overboard so they wash ashore. But he finally found one of each and strung them up on the line to dry. Help him find each sock's match. Then write the letter on each match to spell out the answer to the riddle.

What kind of socks does a pirate wear?

Art by Josh Cleland

The Lost Sock

You can read this to yourself or gather friends and family to perform this as a puppet show!

Narrator

Blue Sock

Red Sock 1

Red Sock 2

Narrator: Once upon a time, there were three little socks.

Blue Sock: Don't you mean once upon a foot?

Narrator: I guess you could put it that way. . . .

Red Sock 1: There was a red sock.

Blue Sock: A blue sock.

Red Sock 2: And another red sock.

Red Sock 1 and Red Sock 2: We make a great pair. *(They giggle.)*

Narrator: The red socks did indeed make a great pair. They went everywhere together. And when they weren't out and about, they nestled in the sock drawer as a sock ball. *(The red socks snore.)* The blue sock, meanwhile, was all alone, which made him feel . . . well, blue.

Blue Sock: Of course I'm blue! I'm a blue sock.

Narrator: I mean blue as in sad because the other blue sock is gone.

Blue Sock: True, I am blue. But I'm not sad. I have a lot of time to myself now that I'm not part of a pair.

Red Sock 1 and Red Sock 2: We like being teammates. Red, red, go red! *(The red socks jump up and down.)*

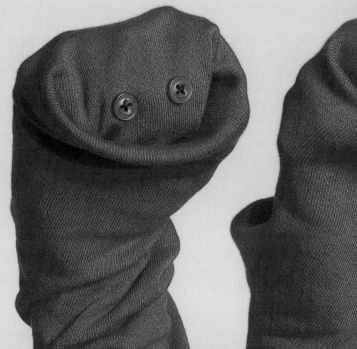

miss my brother sock. I don't know where he went. I don't know what happened to him.

Red Sock 2: Please don't cry, Blue Sock. You might shrink. We don't want you to be sad. Why don't you pair up with me one day?

Red Sock 1: And you can pair up with me one day, too!

Blue Sock: You mean it? You're not afraid people will laugh at us?

Red Sock 1 and Red Sock 2: No! You're our cousin.

Red Sock 1, Red Sock 2, and Blue Sock: Sock Power!

Narrator: And so the blue sock paired up with the red socks for a time, but he was still lonely without his brother.

Blue Sock: Well, I don't have to worry about being stepped on all day long by smelly feet.

Red Sock 2: We love being on feet. After a day on smelly feet, we get to go for the best ride around.

Red Sock 1: And she means around and around and around.

Red Sock 1 and Red Sock 2: In the washing machine. *Whee!*

Blue Sock: That is fun. And I do miss the dryer, getting all warm and fluffy. *(Pauses.)* Gee, I guess I am missing out by not being part of a team. *(Sighs, now sad.)* I do

Blue Sock: I must find him. He is my "sole mate."

Narrator: So the socks went looking for the missing blue sock.

Red Sock 1: He's not here under the bed.

Red Sock 2: He's not here in the bottom of the laundry bag.

Narrator: They even looked in the sock drawers of the other people in the house.

Blue Sock: Where could he be? I hope the cat didn't get him.

Narrator: Then the socks heard the whirr and hum of a sewing machine.

Blue Sock: The sewing machine. Now I remember! My brother was in an accident and got a hole in his toe. He needed stitches!

Narrator: And so the socks hurried off to the sewing machine. There they found Blue Sock's brother being mended. The search for the missing sock was a resounding . . .

Red Sock 1, Red Sock 2, and Blue Sock: Sock-sess!

The End

By Jeffrey B. Fuerst • Art by Paula Becker
Photos by Nannette Bedway

Brain Starters

START HERE

Take your brain on a hike.
How far can you go?

What silly sock designs
would you make?

Name
3
uses for a
single sock.

Why are
socks and pants
separate pieces
of clothing
instead of
attached to
each other?

What do you put on first,
a **sock** or a **shoe**?

When do you wear
silly socks?

What other
articles of clothing
are similar to socks?

Where
might you see
a **sock** besides
on a **foot**?

THE
END

Which sock colors do
you wear the most?
WHY?

Why don't we
wear socks on
our hands the
way we do on
our feet?

What other
things can you
wear on
your feet?

Art by Dave Klug, Erin Mauterer, and Kevin Zimmer • Photos by iStock

110

Sock Search

Can you find 10 socks in this picture?

Art by Mary Sullivan

Sock Code

There are three jokes about socks on this page.
Use the picture code to fill in the letters and finish the jokes.

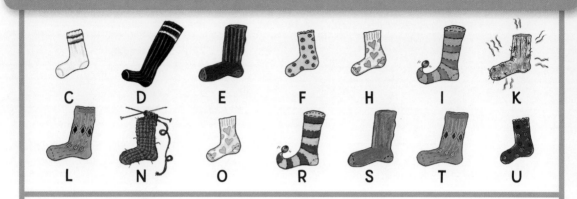

Why was the elephant walking around in socks?

Did you hear the joke about the gym sock?

Why did the monster knit three socks?

Art by Sharon Vargo

Monster Sock Puppets

1. For a face, cut out a circle from **cardstock**. Glue on **yarn** for **fur**, **pompom** eyes with **felt** pupils, a **balloon** nose, and a **rickrack** mouth. Glue the face to the toe of an old sock.

2. For armholes, cut a slit in each side of the sock below the head. Put an **old glove** inside the sock, with the thumb and pinky finger sticking out of the slits.

3. For claws, glue rickrack to the end of each arm.

4. For a tail, pinch a bit of fabric on the back of the puppet. Poke a **chenille stick** through the fabric and twist it in place. Bend or curl the tail.

5. Make a few puppets, and put on a show!

Use a couch or desk as a stage, or make your own!

Hidden Pieces

Can you find the 8 jigsaw pieces below in this photo of socks?

A Hole New Word

It's time to get crafty. Use letters in the words **SOCK PUPPET** to spell new, shorter words. For example, the words SOUP and STOP are both in there. See how many other words you can create.

SOCK PUPPET

soup

_____

stop

_____

_____

_____

_____

_____

_____

_____

_____

_____

_____

_____

_____

What's Wrong?®

What things in this picture are silly? It's up to you!

Word Ladders

It's time to get dressed. But it looks like your clothes are changing themselves! Can you help each item change into another? Use the clues to fill in the blanks. Each word is only one letter different from the word above it.

Puzzle 1

1. "Take your best ___."

2. Dirt from a chimney

S H O E
S H O T
_ _ _ _
B O O T

Puzzle 2

1. A stone

2. A chess piece

3. Make a recipe

4. Opposite of warm

5. Santa might give a lump of this.

S O C K
_ _ _ _
_ _ _ _
_ _ _ _
_ _ _ _
_ _ _ _
C O A T

Puzzle 3

1. Frighten

2. Let a friend play with your toys.

3. The beach

4. Not tall

S C A R F
_ _ _ _ _
_ _ _ _ _
_ _ _ _ _
_ _ _ _ _
S H I R T

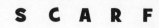

Art by Kelly Kennedy

Sock Stumper

A Game for Two or More Players

To Play:

1. Gather five clean tube socks.
2. Look around your home for five small objects—one to place inside each sock. (Don't use anything sharp or fragile!)
3. Have your friends reach inside the socks and try to guess what the objects are.
4. Take turns filling the socks with different items.

For More Fun:
- Feel the objects from outside the sock instead of reaching inside.
- Place all of the objects in one sock.

Try using these objects to stump your friends!
- Rock
- Twist tie
- Hair elastic
- Unopened bandage
- Plastic bottle cap
- Clean tissue

By Tamara C. Gureghian • Art by Pierre Collet-Derby

Tongue Twisters

Say each one three times, fast!

Oksana wants some awesome socks.

See Shawn's shoe shelf? Shambles!

Steph's pink sock stinks.

Art by Kevin Zimmer

119

Sock Shop Path

These clothes keep piling up. Use the key to make it through the store and to the counter to purchase some snazzy new socks!

Move 1 space **DOWN**

Move 1 space **LEFT**

Move 1 space **RIGHT**

Move 1 space **UP**

Path 1	Path 2	Path 3	Path 4	Path 5	Path 6

120

Art by Mike Moran

Foot Funnies

What does it mean when you find a horseshoe?
Some poor horse is walking around in just his socks.

Rose: What do you wear on your foot besides a sock?
Bob: A shoe.
Rose: Bless you!

What do you call a ball that wears a sock?
A football.

Ned: Why are you taking off your sock?
Ben: My foot is asleep.
Ned: How will taking off your sock help?
Ben: It will make my foot less cozy.

Beth: Do you have holes in your socks?
Jeff: No.
Beth: Then how do you get your feet in them?

What did one sock say to its partner?
"You're my sole mate."

Why couldn't the two socks get along?
Because they both thought they were right.

What did the socks say to the hat?
"You go on a-head. I'll follow you on foot!"

Where does a dog wash his socks?
At a laundro-mutt.

Art by Rich Powell and Kevin Rechin

Socks for the Whole Family

Sam loves his new socks so much, he decided to buy a pair for each of his family members. Can you figure out which pair of socks Sam bought for which family member?

Can you find the candle, comb, horn, pumpkin, and teacup?

Art by Guy Francis

1. The two females got socks that had a color in common.

2. Sam's mom gave Jonah a plaid hat to match the socks Sam gave him.

3. Sam gave his sister socks with her school colors—blue and white.

4. Sam's dad did not get socks with any orange on them.

Use the chart to keep track of your answers. Put an X in each box that can't be true and an O in boxes that match.

	white-and-blue stripes	solid green	red-and-black plaid	blue-and-yellow polka dots	orange animal print
Mom					
Dad					
Jonah					
Ava					
Grandpa					

Knit Pick

Follow the yarn to see what everyone is knitting.

What's Wrong?®

Which things in this picture are silly? It's up to you!

Art by Joey Ellis

Check . . . and Double Check

Compare these two pictures. Can you find at least 15 differences?

S-S-Socks!

Stinky space socks and *Scout steals socks* both have three words that start with the letter S. What silly phrase can you think of that can be described with three *S* words? Draw a picture of it here.

Art by Donna Catanese and Kevin Rechin

Sock Animals

Sock Penguin

1. Stuff the toe of a sock with a paper napkin.

2. Slide the sock over the bottom of a paper cup. Tuck the rest of the sock inside the cup.

3. Glue on wiggle eyes and details cut from colored paper or felt, as shown.

Sock Bunny

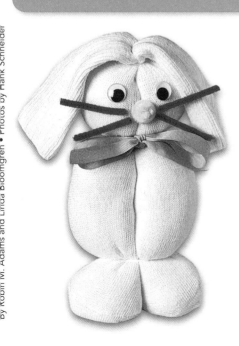

1. Stuff the foot part of two socks with fiberfill or cotton balls.

2. With string, tie the socks together in three places to create feet, a body, a head, and ears.

3. Glue on wiggle eyes, a pompom nose, whiskers made from chenille sticks, and a tail made from a cotton ball. Tie a ribbon around the bunny's neck.

What other animals can you make out of socks?

By Robin M. Adams and Linda Bloomgren • Photos by Hank Schneider

Missing Socks

Socks are always getting lost in the laundromat.
Can you find the 20 socks hidden in this scene?

Art by Dave Klug

129

At the Sock Hop

Four pairs of socks in this scene have an exact match. Can you find all the matching pairs? There are also seven words hidden in this scene. Can you find HOP, SOCK, DANCE, SONG, ROCK, SWING, and MUSIC?

Art by Kelly Kennedy

In the 1950s, informal dances were often held in school gyms or cafeterias. Dancers were asked to remove their shoes to protect the floor, so these dances became known as *sock hops.*

Answers

Page 2

Page 3

Page 4

Page 5

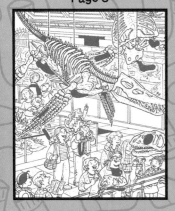

Page 6

Page 7

Page 8

Page 9

Page 10

Answers

Page 11

Page 12

Page 13

Page 14

Page 15

Page 16

Page 17

Page 18
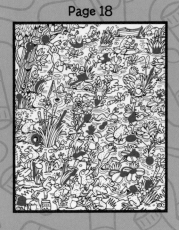

Page 19

Page 20

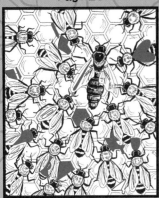

Page 21

Page 22

Page 23

Page 24

Page 25

Page 26

Page 27

Page 28

Answers

Page 29

Page 30

Page 31

Page 32

Page 33

Page 34

Page 35

Page 36

Page 37

Page 38

Page 39

Page 40

Page 41

Page 42

Page 43

Page 44

Page 45

Page 46

Answers

Page 47

Page 48

Page 49

Page 50

Page 51

Page 52

Page 53

Page 54

Page 55

Answers

Page 56

Page 57

Page 58

Page 59

Page 60

Page 61

Page 62

Page 63

Page 64

Answers

Page 65

Page 66

Page 67

Page 68

Page 69

Page 70

Page 71

Page 72

Page 73

Page 74

Page 75

Page 76

Page 77

Page 78

Page 79

Page 80

Page 81

Page 82

Answers

Page 83

Page 84

Page 85

Page 86

Page 87

Page 88

Page 89

Page 90

Page 91

Answers

Page 92

Page 93

Page 94

Page 95

Page 96

Page 97

- We found 1 T-shirt, 2 pairs of pants, and 8 shoes. You may have found other things you wear.
- We found 13 mittens and 19 gloves. There are more gloves.
- The spools of thread are on pages 23, 32, 47, 54, 67, 71, 79, 90, and 92.

Pages 98—99

Page 100

Answers

Page 101

Page 103

Page 104

Leo: Monster Socks;
Most Creative

Hazel: Monkey Socks;
Best Overall

Wyatt: Popcorn Socks;
Silliest

Nora: Cow Socks;
Scariest

Eli: Superhero Socks;
Funniest

Page 105

Page 106

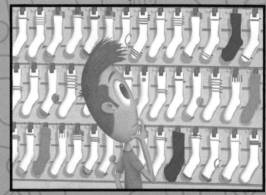

Page 107

Page 111

Page 112

Why was the elephant
walking around in socks?
HE COULDN'T FIND HIS
SHOES.

Did you hear the joke
about the gym sock?
IT STINKS.

Why did the monster knit
three socks?
FOR HIS THREE FEET

Answers

Pages 114—115

Page 116

Here are some words we found in SOCK PUPPET. You may have found others.

COP, COST, CUE, CUP, CUPS, CUSP, CUT, CUTE, CUTS, OUT, PECK, PET, PETS, POCKET, POCKETS, POKE, POP, POSE, POST, POTS, POUT, PUCK, PUP, PUT, SCOUT, SPOKE, SPOT, SPOUT, STEP, STOCK, TOP, TUCK

Page 118

SHOE	SCARF
SHOT	SCARE
SOOT	SHARE
BOOT	SHORE
	SHORT
SOCK	SHIRT
ROCK	
ROOK	
COOK	
COOL	
COAL	
COAT	

Page 120

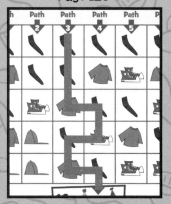

Page 122 (top)

Page 122 (bottom)

Mom: blue-and-yellow polka dots

Dad: solid green

Jonah: red-and-black plaid

Ava: white-and-blue stripes

Grandpa: orange animal print

Page 123

Answers

Page 125

Pages 128—129

Page 130

For information about permission to reproduce
selections from this book, please contact
permissions@highlights.com.

Published by Highlights for Children
P.O. Box 18201
Columbus, Ohio 43218-0201
Printed in China
ISBN: 978-1-68437-170-9

First edition
Visit our website at Highlights.com.
10 9 8 7 6 5 4 3 2 1